P9-BBV-184

ZAMBIA

IS MY HOME

For a free color catalog describing Gareth Stevens' list of high-quality books, call 1-800-341-3569 (USA) or 1-800-461-9120 (Canada).

For their help in the preparation of *My Home Country: Zambia Is My Home,* the editors gratefully thank the Embassy of Zambia, Washington, DC; the United States Department of State, Bureau of Public Affairs, Office of Public Communications, Washington, DC, for the unencumbered use of material in the public domain; Meg Skinner, International Student Office, University of Wisconsin-Madison; and Stella Semiti. The author and photographer would like to thank the United States Department of State, Bureau of Consular Affairs; Don Murray of the Christian Children's Fund, the Boston University Department of African Studies; Father Noel Brennan of Livingstone; Sister Ann and the Franciscan Missionary Sisters of Africa; Phyllis Palmer of Ker Downey Selby in Maun, Botswana; and Betty Wessels of SATOUR in Pretoria, South Africa.

Flag illustration on page 42, © Flag Research Center.

Library of Congress Cataloging-in-Publication Data

Karpfinger, Beth.
    Zambia is my home / adapted from Barbara Radcliffe Rogers' Children of the world : Zambia by Beth Karpfinger ; photographs by Stillman Rogers.
        p.   cm. — (My home country)
    Summary: Presents the life of a thirteen-year-old girl and her family in Zambia, describing her home and school activities and discussing the history, geography, people, government, economy, and culture of her country.
        ISBN 0-8368-0906-8
    [1. Zambia. 2. Family life—Zambia.] I. Rogers, Barbara Radcliffe. Zambia. II. Title. III. Series.
DT3052.K37   1993
968.94—dc20
                                                                                    92-30686

BT 18.60/14.88 8/95

Edited, designed, and produced by

Gareth Stevens Publishing
1555 North RiverCenter Drive, Suite 201
Milwaukee, Wisconsin   53212, USA

Text, photographs, and format © 1993 by Gareth Stevens, Inc. First published in the United States and Canada in 1993 by Gareth Stevens, Inc. This US edition is abridged from *Children of the World: Zambia,* © 1991 by Gareth Stevens, Inc., with text by Barbara Radcliffe Rogers and photographs by Stillman Rogers.

Series editors: Barbara J. Behm and Beth Karpfinger
Cover design: Kristi Ludwig
Layout: Beth Karpfinger
Map design: Sheri Gibbs

Printed in the United States of America

1 2 3 4 5 6 7 8 9 96 95 94 93 92

My Home Country

ZAMBIA
IS MY HOME

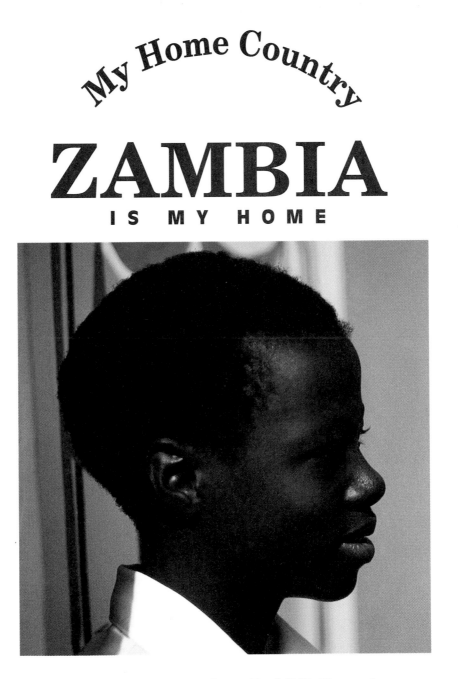

Adapted from Barbara Radcliffe Rogers'
Children of the World: Zambia

by Beth Karpfinger
Photographs by Stillman Rogers

Gareth Stevens Publishing
MILWAUKEE

Christabel Mooka is a 13-year-old girl from Livingstone, Zambia, in southern Africa. She lives with her older sister, Theresa, and Theresa's baby, Namakau. Christabel helps her sister with household chores, including child care, cooking, and gardening. She is also a weaver, and she makes beautiful baskets from reeds and grasses growing near her home. Christabel is an excellent student, and English is her favorite subject. For fun, she visits the Mosi-oa-Tunya National Park to see animals roaming in the wild.

To enhance this book's value in libraries and classrooms, clear and simple reference sections include up-to-date information about Zambia's history, land and climate, people and language, education, and religion. *Zambia Is My Home* also features a large and colorful map, bibliography, glossary, simple index, research topics, and activity projects designed especially for young readers.

The living conditions and experiences of children in Zambia vary according to economic, environmental, and ethnic circumstances. The reference sections help bring to life for young readers the diversity and richness of the culture and heritage of Zambia. Of particular interest are discussions of Zambia's government, natural resources, cultural life, and its long and exciting history.

My Home Country includes the following titles:

Canada	*Nicaragua*
Costa Rica	*Peru*
Cuba	*Poland*
El Salvador	*South Africa*
Guatemala	*Vietnam*
Ireland	*Zambia*

CONTENTS

"Mapona! [Hello!] My name is Christabel, and I live in Zambia."

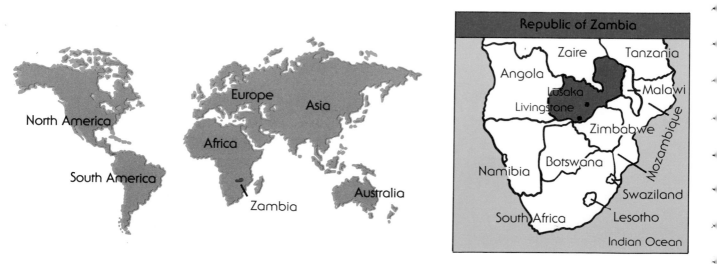

North America

South America

Europe

Asia

Africa

Zambia

Australia

Republic of Zambia

Zaire

Tanzania

Angola

Lusaka

Malawi

Livingstone

Zimbabwe

Mozambique

Namibia

Botswana

Swaziland

South Africa

Lesotho

Indian Ocean

6

LIVING IN ZAMBIA:
Christabel, a Girl from Livingstone

Christabel Mooka is a 13-year-old girl from Zambia, a country in southern Africa. She lives in Livingstone, a city on the border between the countries of Zambia and Zimbabwe.

Christabel is the youngest of seven brothers and three sisters. She lives with her older sister, Theresa, and Theresa's son, Namakau. Christabel moved to Theresa's house three years ago so that she could attend Saint Mary's Seminary School.

Christabel's older sister with her son, Namakau.

Even though Christabel lives with her sister, she sees her mother, Cecelia Mwitumwa, often. However, Christabel rarely sees her father, who runs a market in an area called the Western Province.

Many Zambian families live apart. Men usually leave their homes in the villages to find work elsewhere to support their families. Children often live in the homes of relatives who can afford to raise them. Theresa is a teacher, and she is able to pay for Christabel's school fees and clothes.

Christabel with her sister, nephew, aunt, and mother.

Christabel's mother helps Theresa put Namakau on her back.

The home Christabel shares with Theresa and Namakau has only two small rooms. Christabel and Theresa cook, eat, study, and visit with friends in their yard. They use the house for sleeping and for shelter when it rains. Their house looks like those of their neighbors, with cement walls and a tin roof.

◀ **Christabel's house is built of brightly painted cement blocks.**

Livingstone's red dirt streets do not create much dust. The only time dust forms is when children play ball in the street.

The children have made a ball by tying rags together.

The Zambezi River flows so smoothly past Livingstone that
it is hard to believe that the river will soon drop over a cliff.

Namakau bounces along on his mother's back.

Christabel makes breakfast.

Christabel's School Day

At 6:00 a.m., the big, white alarm clock wakes everyone with its loud ringing. While Theresa bathes Namakau, Christabel cooks porridge on a stove in the yard. After breakfast, Theresa takes Namakau to Cecelia's house. She then goes to the school where she teaches. Christabel walks to school alone. Classes begin at 7:30 a.m.

Saint Mary's is one of Zambia's finest schools. The girls are proud of its motto.

MARAMBA

KNOWLEDGE ◆ LOVE ◆ SERVICE

Christabel likes to arrive
early to talk with her friends.

Saint Mary's Seminary School is a private school for girls. Most people in Zambia agree that it is the best school in the country. That is why Christabel's mother and sister wanted her to go there. About half the girls at Saint Mary's are from other parts of Zambia and must live at school.

All of the students in Christabel's class had to pass a test to get into the eighth grade.

It feels good to be outside between morning classes.

Some of the nuns who run the school are Zambian, and others are British. The principal, Sister Ann, is from Scotland. Most of the teachers are not nuns.

The school building has a row of classrooms around a large, grassy courtyard.

Sister Ann has lived in Zambia for over four years.

Mr. Katanga is Christabel's eighth grade teacher.

Christabel listens carefully.

Mr. Katanga is Christabel's teacher. Nearly 40 girls crowd into the small classroom. It is not noisy because Mr. Katanga makes the subjects interesting. Mr. Katanga teaches most subjects without books because

books are scarce. Christabel writes everything he says in her notebook. She also carefully copies maps and diagrams from the blackboard into her notebook.

From 10:00 to 10:15, Christabel's class has recess. The girls get together to laugh and to talk about the day's events.

Some girls bring snacks to eat with their morning tea.

Christabel's favorite subject is English, which she has studied since she started school. Christabel also studies math, science, home economics, religion, geography, social studies, and art.

With so many subjects, the school day is long. But Christabel doesn't mind working hard because she wants to become a nurse.

Zambian children sing this song about the long hours and hard work at school:

Let me come in!
Don't come in!
Let me come in!
Don't come in!
School is hard,
It is not for lazy people,
People who do not wake up early.
Open the door. Let me come in.

◄ **Christabel enjoys a moment of sunshine outside her school.**

Sister Ann thinks that cooking skills are important. Jobs are scarce in Zambia, especially for girls, so she wants them to have as many skills as possible.

◀ In home economics class, Christabel learns how to cook.

The teachers test the students on their cooking skills.

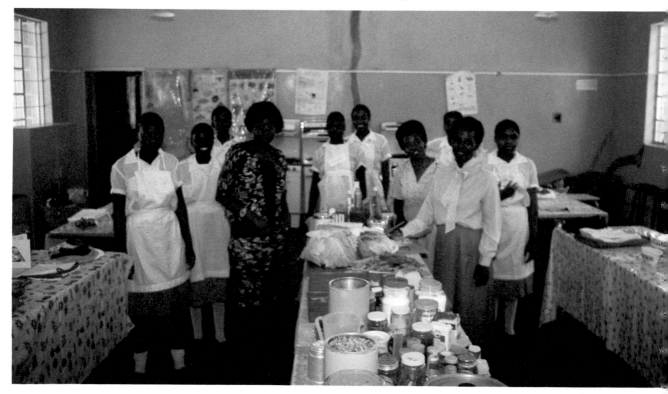

In home economics, Christabel and her classmates prepare a meal and serve it at a table.   But in most homes, families eat while sitting on grass mats outside.

The students are graded on how nicely they arrange the food.

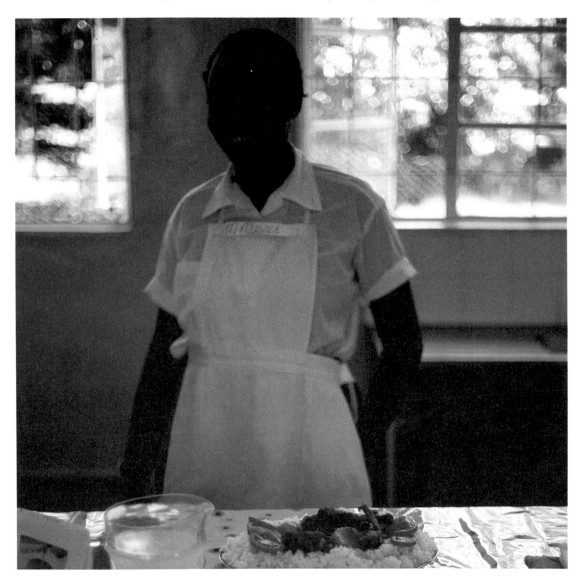

Above: Mr. Kapenda teaches gardening.
Left: St. Mary's has its own well.

The School Garden

Saint Mary's has a large garden where the vegetables and fruits served at the school are raised. All schools have gardens to teach the students how to grow food.

Christabel works in the garden during two class periods each week, learning to plant and care for the many fruits and vegetables. Even though working with a hoe and a shovel is hard work in the hot sun, Christabel enjoys this break from the classroom.

The chicken house beside the school garden is empty now but will soon have a flock of baby chicks. The girls will learn how to raise them for meat and eggs.

Cabbages grow well in the soil near the Zambezi River.

The girls learn to use water sparingly, since they have to carry it in buckets from the well.

Mr. Kapenda teaches Christabel gardening and art. Christabel looks forward to Mr. Kapenda's art class. She learns crafts, such as macramé and weaving. Christabel has even learned how to find plants that can be used as materials to make crafts.

Christabel hangs her macramé project on a line to keep it from getting tangled.

This classmate's basket is nearly finished.

The reeds and grasses that Christabel has gathered must be soaked in the sink to make them soft enough to weave.

Christabel collects reeds and grasses along the banks of the Zambezi River and brings them back to the classroom. She soaks them in a large sink to soften them. She then weaves them into baskets.

After School with Christabel

After school, Christabel changes from her school uniform into a dress. In Zambia, girls never wear shorts or slacks.

Christabel does her homework outside. When she is reading, she sits on a grass mat in the yard. When she needs to write, Christabel brings the table from the house outside and uses it as a desk.

The porch has more light for studying. ▸
Below: Christabel has copied maps from the blackboard.

Sometimes Christabel has to look after Namakau. Even for young girls, doing chores and watching children is women's work in Zambia. Most boys are given lots of free time to play. But girls like Christabel cannot spend much time with friends.

Late in the afternoon, Christabel's mother, aunts, and older sisters may stop by for a

"Swing me around!"

"Please water the flowers,"
Theresa reminds Christabel.

The relatives take off their shoes when they sit on the grass mat.

visit. They sit on the grass mats under the tree in the front yard and talk. Theresa often feeds Namakau as she sits with her mother and aunts.

Christabel's Garden

Christabel's favorite hobby is taking care of the flower garden in front of her home. She pulls the weeds, picks off the dead flowers, and keeps the plants healthy. She uses the skills she has learned from Mr. Kapenda.

A tall papaya tree grows in Theresa's yard. ▸
Below: Christabel's flower garden brightens the yard.

Two Customs of Zambia

Nearly every meal Christabel eats includes a dish called mealies. Mealies are white corn kernels that are dried and ground, then cooked with milk or water.

Almost every family has a mealie pounder, a large wooden mortar and pestle with which the dried corn is pounded. Christabel's mother grinds corn in one of these every day. She sits on a low stool, working the pounder up and down to crush the corn. The thump-thump of the mealie pounder has always been a part of Christabel's life.

Right: Mealies are similar to white corn grits.
Opposite: One of Christabel's earliest memories is of her mother pounding mealies.

Livingstone: A Special City

Livingstone is one of the oldest cities in Zambia. It is named after Dr. David Livingstone, a British explorer.

In Livingstone, the Zambezi River spills over a long cliff and drops 300 feet (91 m) to form Victoria Falls. The mist from the falls can be seen from 20 miles (32 km) away. People throughout the world come to see this natural wonder.

A statue of Dr. Livingstone (left) at Victoria Falls (opposite).

On the weekends, Christabel goes to Mosi-oa-Tunya National Park. The park is an animal reserve on the banks of the Zambezi River. People walk along the riverbanks and can see zebras, wildebeests, impalas, waterbuck, and Cape buffalo. Christabel feels proud to live in an area of the world that is so special.

Top: Monkeys sit in trees along the road.

Bottom: Signs warn motorists to make way for the animals.

Opposite: Baobab trees dot the grasslands, known as savannas.

MORE FACTS ABOUT: Zambia

Official Name: Republic of Zambia
(ZAM-bee-uh)

Capital: Lusaka

History

About 2,000 years ago, Bantu-speaking peoples from northern Africa began migrating into Zambia. By the 7th century AD, these people were trading with Arabs. They traded ivory, rhinoceros horns, copper, and even slaves captured from other tribes.

In the late 1880s, Cecil Rhodes began to excavate minerals in Zambia. Rhodes was the head of the British South Africa Company (BSAC). As more Europeans arrived to work the mines, divisions between blacks and whites increased. The British government took farmland away from blacks and gave it to white settlers. During this time, a group of black Africans began working for more rights for blacks. In 1949, blacks formed the Northern Rhodesia African Mine Workers' Union. In 1958, the Zambian African National Congress (ZANC) formed. Kenneth Kaunda was elected president of the ZANC. In 1963, the ZANC and the United

National Independent Party (UNIP) joined to form Zambia's first black government. On October 23, 1964, the BSAC gave up its rights to Zambia. Zambia then became an independent nation with Kaunda as its president. Kaunda has been president of Zambia since 1964. All political parties except his own have been outlawed, and the military prevents any protests against the failing economy of Zambia.

Land and Climate

Most of Zambia is a plateau 3,000 to 5,000 feet (914 to 1,524 m) high, covered by grassy savanna. In winter, temperatures range from 60° to 80°F (16° to 27°C). In the summer, temperatures range from 80° to 100°F (27° to 38°C).

People and Language

Zambia's seven million people are made up of four major ethnic groups. These are the Lozi, the Bemba, the Lunda, and the Ngoni. English is the official language of Zambia, but most Zambians speak their native languages at home and in school.

Religion

About 60% of Zambians are Christians, and most of these are Roman Catholics. The remaining 40% practice tribal religions.

Education

When Zambia became independent, the entire country had only 100 black college graduates, and only 3% of the population had attended primary school.

The kwacha is the unit of money in Zambia.

Despite these problems, the number of children in high school rose from 14,000 in 1964 to 114,000 in 1984. Some children do not attend school because they live in villages that have no schools or because their families cannot afford the fees.

Sports and Recreation

Soccer is Zambia's most popular team sport. Along with soccer, other favorite competitive sports are rugby and squash. Zambians also play an ancient board game called *chisolo*.

Zambians in North America

About 750 Zambians live in the United States and Canada. Many of them are college students who left Zambia because space at the University of Zambia is very limited. In North America, they usually attend the universities that have African studies programs.

Glossary of Useful Zambian (Tonga) Terms:

mapona (mah POH-nah): hello

muli kabutu (MOO-lee kah-BOO-too): how are you?

nda lumba (en-dah LUHM-bah): thank you

More Books about Zambia

Enchantment of the World: Zambia. Laure
  (Childrens Press)
The Land and People of Zambia. Dresang
  (Lippincott)

Things to Do

1. In Zambia, the Mosi-oa-Tunya National Park is home to many wild animals. Go to a zoo near your home. Make a list of the animals from Zambia.

2. If you would like to have a Zambian pen pal, write to: Worldwide Pen Friends, P.O. Box 39097, Downey, CA 90241

Be sure to tell them what country you want your pen pal to be from. Also include your full name, age, and address.

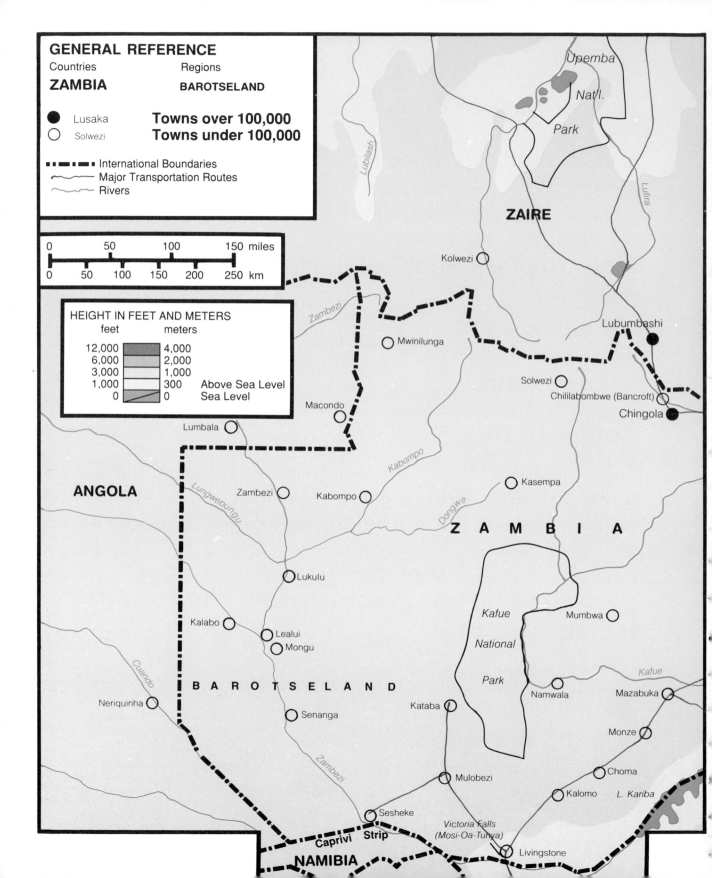

GENERAL REFERENCE

Countries	Regions
ZAMBIA	**BAROTSELAND**

● Lusaka   **Towns over 100,000**
○ Solwezi   **Towns under 100,000**

■-■-■ International Boundaries
〜 Major Transportation Routes
〜 Rivers

0	50	100	150 miles
0	50	100	150	200	250 km

HEIGHT IN FEET AND METERS
feet	meters	
12,000	4,000	
6,000	2,000	
3,000	1,000	
1,000	300	Above Sea Level
0	0	Sea Level

Upemba

Nat'l.

Park

Lubilash

Lufira

ZAIRE

Kolwezi ○

Lubumbashi ○

Zambezi

Mwinilunga ○

Solwezi ○

Chililabombwe (Bancroft) ○

Chingola ●

Macondo ○

Lumbala ○

Kabompo

ANGOLA

Lungwebungu

Zambezi ○

Kabompo ○

Kasempa ○

Dongwe

Z A M B I A

Lukulu ○

Kafue

National

Park

Mumbwa ○

Kalabo ○

Lealui ○
Mongu ○

Cuando

B A R O T S E L A N D

Namwala ○

Kafue

Mazabuka ○

Kataba ○

Monze ○

Neriquinha ○

Senanga ○

Zambezi

Choma ○

Kalomo ○

L. Kariba

Mulobezi ○

Sesheke ○

Caprivi **Strip**

Victoria Falls (Mosi-Oa-Tunya)

Livingstone ○

NAMIBIA

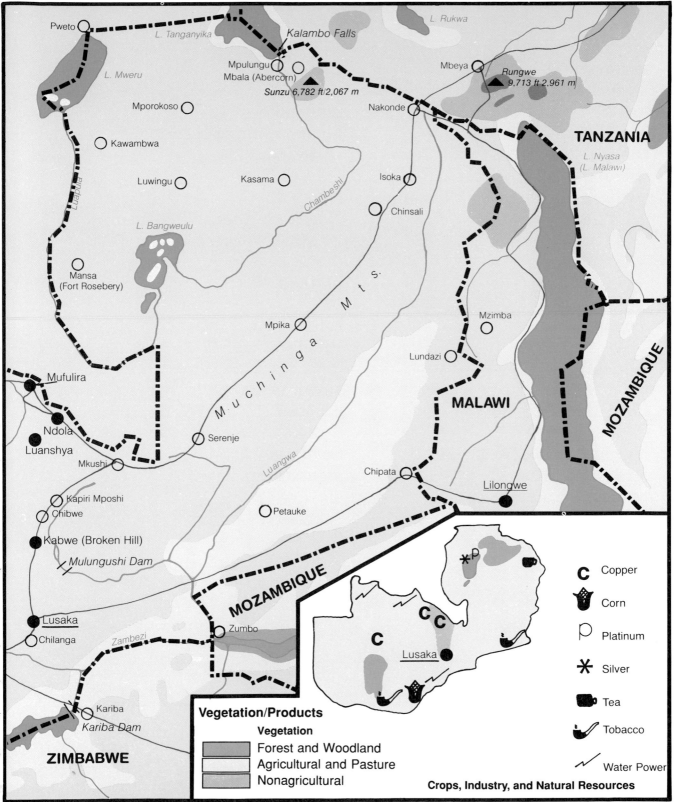

ZAMBIA — Political and Physical

Pweto
L. Tanganyika
Kalambo Falls
L. Rukwa
Mpulungu
Mbala (Abercorn)
Sunzu 6,782 ft/2,067 m
L. Mweru
Mporokoso
Kawambwa
Luwingu
Kasama
Chambeshi
Isoka
Chinsali
Mbeya
Rungwe
9,713 ft 2,961 m
Nakonde
TANZANIA
L. Nyasa
(L. Malawi)
Luapula
L. Bangweulu
Mansa
(Fort Rosebery)
Mpika
M u c h i n g a   M t s.
Mzimba
Lundazi
MALAWI
MOZAMBIQUE
Mufulira
Ndola
Luanshya
Mkushi
Serenje
Luangwa
Chipata
Lilongwe
Kapiri Mposhi
Chibwe
Kabwe (Broken Hill)
Mulungushi Dam
Petauke
MOZAMBIQUE
Lusaka
Chilanga
Zambezi
Zumbo
Kariba
Kariba Dam
ZIMBABWE

Vegetation/Products

Vegetation

▨	Forest and Woodland
☐	Agricultural and Pasture
▨	Nonagricultural

C Copper

🌽 Corn

○ Platinum

✳ Silver

▨ Tea

🚬 Tobacco

⟋ Water Power

Crops, Industry, and Natural Resources

Inset map labels: *P, C, C, C, Lusaka*

Index